Finding Myself

a collection of poems

noor afasa

BookLeaf Publishing

India | USA | UK

Made with ❤ on the BookLeaf Publishing Platform
www.bookleafpub.in
www.bookleafpub.com

Dedication

To those who make life better,
I appreciate you.
I pray you are always happy and healthy
Ameen

Preface

This book includes 21 poems that have been written in 21 days, and so although these poems won't be the best, edited versions, I am grateful to be able to share them. Thank you for choosing to read my poetry - it means a lot!

In this book, I have wrote poems without actually putting too much thought to what I should write about but instead, what naturally comes to me, which has been very nice and reflective. I hope you enjoy your read!

Acknowledgements

Thank you to everyone who has come into my life,
bringing even the slightest bit of happiness.

Family and friends, thank you for endlessly giving me
your love and support. You are always in my duas.

I want to thank the Performance Collective for inspiring
me but also, always making me feel like an inspiration.

And Safa, thank you so much. Thank you for being such a
good friend and always being the first to read my poems.

Last but certainly not least, my Ammi. No matter how
many times I say 'thank you', I could never thank you
enough. I may not say it as much as I should, but I love
and appreciate you more than words could ever express.
Thank you for believing in me and supporting me.

1. accent

me and my dad don't speak the same language
and, neither do we share the same accent.
our r's roll of our tongues in different ways:
mine comes easily and natural,
his, shy and hesitant.
not because he struggles to say it
but, because he thinks twice
before saying it in front of you.
because his r's come from a rural village,
from karak chai,
from the roundness of rotis,
and an unwritten language,
whilst
your r is the one in ignorance
in front of which,
my fathers r rolls up, bends, bows and shrivels in shame.
in front of which,
his voice becomes
small.
because you only hear those

who speak like you do.
because you don't like how his words sound,
because when i stretched your moth
and pulled the alphabet out,
ignorance is the only thing i found.

2. the echo of bangles

when my bangles jingle,
they sound just like my grandma's.
and they shine just like hers do,
round and reflecting the sunlight, just like the moon.

but when my bangles jingle,
it's not just my grandma's they echo,
but all the women who came before.
women who passed on what they know.

although i am made of those women
and what they know,
and just because our bangles sound and shine in
the same way,
and have done so for so long,
i will not continue the things that we know,
that we know are wrong.

i will not let my bangles sound louder than my voice.

and when i pass mine on,
rather than as shackles on her arms,
i will place them in her palms.

3. my city

i come from a city
with such beautiful history.
the Brontës, Hockney and Priestley.
endless creativity
because we do things differently.

i come from the wool capital of the world,
with some of the most famous mills,
a gateway to the countryside
and the greenest hills.

Bradford.
originally known as 'Broad Ford'
but what are we really known for?
over 120 languages spoken
yet we speak as one.
us Bradfordians welcome you as our own.

i come from a city of film, magic and art -
with people so talented and bold.

our food, unforgettable
our cars, unbeatable
and our spark, unimaginable!

i come from a youthful spirit.
29%, remember that number,
excitement and change,
what's next? i wonder

a city that once thrived,
will thrive once more.
a city with drive,
never seen before.

i come from a city,
making such beautiful history.
i come from Bradford.

4. remembering you

you say to remember you,
so i do.
i carry your name on my tongue
and in my heart,
even carry you in my curved palms.
i call for you
when the silence is loud,
when the night is dark,
and the sun has found rest.

i call for you and the silence remains,
but i know you're listening.
i call for you and i'm alone,
but i know you're there.
and when i don't call for you,
i know you're waiting.

5. drowning

the sound of silence is loud.
it's the waves still and calm,
on shore
but the waves fighting each other
out at sea.
and if i was the ocean, this is how i'd be,
silent and smiling
just how you want me,
but
in the places where you can't reach me,
i would still be screaming
underwater
in hope you'll hear me.

if i was the ocean,
my waves would carry guilt,
because i stay silent when i shouldn't.
i'm scared of the shame that comes with speaking up.
and why speak when you don't listen?

and if i was the ocean,
the waves would whisper to me instead;
'we have been here longer,
we know better.'

because i'm a girl and i'm young
and i know nothing.
but maybe if i was the ocean,
i wouldn't have to scream but
you would come to me.
silently or smiling, it wouldn't matter
because you would sit by me
and

maybe if i was the ocean
you would
willingly listen to me.

6. woman

to be a woman
is to be many a thing.
it's to give
when you can no longer give.
it's your body losing dance
so instead you sing.

7. children of jannah

i don't know how to write this poem,
because i don't know what to say.
usually hope God understands me as i put my hands up
and pray.
but today, as my hands write
i don't want to say i wish this wasn't happening
because God is the best of planners
and at the end of the day,
these are the children of Jannah.

these children suffering an unimaginable pain.
even in their screams,
they take God's name.
and it amazes me
because they don't call it in vain.
they whisper it under rubble, to the dust and to the rain.
the same dust that will rise and testify on the day
of these children's unwavering faith.
they speak it with such admirable confidence and
strength.

these children with love for their God
and strength bigger than their little bodies.
like they know He is listening,
because they know there's better rewards for their
suffering.

and i promise to not complain,
because the difference between me and them
is pure luck.

because as i stand and wash the dishe,
i look out of the window and try to imagine.
how i would feel
what it would look like
maybe how i'd scream
if i saw bombs dropping from the sky
but forget feelings, i can't even imagine what that would
look like.
and it breaks my heart that this is daily, an every day
all they know
for the children in Palestine.
the children of paradise.

8. lock me in a jar

lock me in a jar
and leave me on your shelf.
so you can pick it up
and show me to your friends.
breathe on the glass
and scrub with your sleeve,
making sure you can clearly see.
and if i try to hide
pull the lid tight
so i can't breathe
and will give in, letting you see.
or poke your finger in
and force up my chin,
or pluck a hair
and threaten me "if you dare".
snatch all the other women you see
and place them in jars next to me.
because it wasn't just me you stared at alone,
but you stared at us all.
and although no one may hear us from the jars,

let the line of jars tell herstory.

14

9. piece of poetry, piece of me

sometimes i wish,
i could crawl out of my skin
flow into my pen
and become the very ink,
that fills page after page
of things i struggle, i'm unable,
i can't bring myself to say.

i wish you'd realise
that words have writers
and these words are written
written by,
me.
i'm not writing a story
something for you to nod and clap at.
neither is it about me performing for you whilst you sit
back
but a piece of poetry
is a piece of me

and when i say read this,
i'm letting you see me.
giving you permission to pick at the seams,
pull out the stitches
and see what lays beneath,
rip back the layers of fabric
so you can see
the very cloth i'm made of
so you understand
that my poetry
is a part of
me.

10. i come from

i come from being ashamed of my tea bag-stained skin,
to being proud of my brown beauty.

i come from a family,
a family who drink chaa four times a day,
who come from a country so beautiful,
yet so corrupt.
a land of spices, samosas and sun.

i come from strong women with strong, mehndi-stained
hands.
intricate designs painted across their palms.
i come from the singing of traditional folk songs,
songs we've heard our mothers,
who've heard their mothers, sing.
i come from a place where us women greet each other -
with a handshake and two pecks,
where the men place a respectful hand on the young
girl's head.

i come from shame, respect and love.
i come from my family, who come from Pakistan.
i come from a culture I love.

11. finding home

when i feel a little lost
and the noise is louder,
when the ground is shaking
and the world feels busier,
the only way to steady myself
is to cross my hands over my chest,
so instead of the noise
i listen to my heart,
and i stand still
in hope that the world will do the same.
and to stop the shaking,
i lay my forehead on thr ground,
eyes closed, and call for my Lord.
whispers so close to the ground
yet, reaching the highest of heavens.
when i feel a little lost,
i try to find
my way back home.

12. death

you lay, peacefully
with a smile on your face
seemingly happy and at ease,
despite the crying and grief
surrounding you.
are you not aware of this pain
or does death turn people selfish?
so many questions i could ask you.
your eyes easily closed
as if you're sleeping,
is that how it feels?
as if any moment now,
your eyes will open.

guilt befriends grief,
because i've already forgotten
what your eyes look like.
whether they shone when you laughed.
i don't think i've ever seen yu c ry,
what did tears look like in your eyes?

they say eyes are a window to the soul,
but where has yours gone?
how can i continue to know you
if your window has now become bolted and shut
boarded up.
i try my hardest to remember staring into them,
i wonder what they looked like
staring into those eyes,
the eyes of death.
did you try fighting back
or did you feel prepared?
did you simply accept
or were you scared?
it's a weird thing to accept i am never going to see you
live, laugh, cry or speak again.

13. brown bodies

our bodies don't look like yours.
a very embarrassing fact,
when i was a little girl.
embarrassed of her thicker hair
and of her darker skin.
i wonder why she believed that
being brown was a sin.

maybe she knew how you looked at her,
sneakily, as though you weren't allowed to.
the way you refused to touch
or befriend her.
or dismissed the correct way to say her name.

and now i've learnt why our bodies aren't the same.
why your backs stay stiff
and head only ever facing straight,
because you know no one is going to come in your way.

our bodies don't move like yours.

mine isn't stiff, it easily falls.
but then i learnt about how it carries a heavy load.
the same heaviness of my ancestors,
the heaviness of your success,
built upon their brown backs.
my brown body doesn't move like yours
because my body comes from those
whose backs bend backwards
upon your call.
who wouldn't bat an eyelash,
who would face the other way,
who would endure all the pain,
because their bodies are wrapped in a different skin.
yet, i believe God made us all of the same clay.

but yes, your body is not like ours.
we share the shine from the sunlight,
our skin outshining our gold.
embodiments of the sunrise itself,
our bodies carry the love of the sun
and stories, untold.

yes, our brown bodies are beautiful
even though they're not like yours at all.

14. what will others think?

sometimes i get excited,
wanting to try new things.
but then i have to look down at my hands,
remind myself of the colour of my skin.
and ask myself,
what will others think?
not that i really care
but *banday keh sochsan*?
suddenly the voice in my head
sasn't my own
but, my voice was whispering somewhere
asking,
who are you living for?

a line that has broken brown hearts too many times.
a line that has stopped so many from living their lives.
because '*banday ke aaksan*?'
what will others say?
a mindset that has stopped parents, grandparents and
generations before,

all asking each other about others,
but let's not stop ourselves anymore,
remind yourself who you're living for.
because
people will always think
and people will always speak
but, i don't want to die
without actually living my life,
because i asked myself wayyy too many times
what will others think?

15. growing up

somewhere between then and now,
a little girl became a woman.

she learnt of her mother's troubles;
she learnt what it means
and, how it feels,
to be a woman.
how hard it must be
to go from living for yourself to living for others.
she finally understood how her mum juggles,
the emotions of her own
but keeps it hidden, so that she is able to first help
others.
help the little girl, her sisters and brother.

and how annoying it must be
when us children think why she's screaming,
over such a little thing
not knowing that there's bigger things
for her to think,

and that, that little scream is nothing
compared to what she's seen
and, how she really feels.

a little girl,
who didn't know any better,
grew up to see
the bittersweet
reality of being a woman.
constantly giving yourself to an ungrateful world
that will only ever,
ask for more.

my mother.
a woman who constantly endures and endures,
to make the world a little better
for her four children.
a woman whose mere silence
is a bigger sacrifice.
what the little girl originally thought was weakness
soon realised,
everything her mum did was
for her children,
to be happier in life.
so for all the women
who have given themselves
to this ungrateful world,

and lost their sense
of who they are,
i want to thank you
for the women you are.

this is a poem for you.

16. untold history

two sides

they say there's two sides to a coin.

and it's the same with history,

every story.

but a side is a side,

and a lie is a lie.

so don't dry up my grandparents tears

with the fabricated lies

you've told for years.

that you've printed on pages

that have taught me about history.

things like britain's industrial revolution.

because my grandad's hands

and quiet mouth

tell a different story.

the cloth that was spun and woven by him

in a Bradford mill,

the fabric that has been made

by his very hands,

gets labelled 'british made',

no trace
of the pakistani hands that gave and gave,
to this country that won't accept his people to this day.
you failed to recognise him as british
and for me who was born here,
you gave me a checklist.
as if to calculate
what percentage of me is truly british.
but let me ask you the same
because britain isn't just britain,
if it's built upon the backs of others.
made up of what you have taken and taken.
if it's built upon the people you called,
who came and gave their all
just to do play their part
in a bigger puppet show,
just to get told
to "go back home"
"where you came from"

but how could you appreciate?
how could you be thankful for my grandad and others
like him?
if instead of seeing
his hard-working, wool-spinning, loving and feeding
hands,
you saw the colour of them first.

so before you paint yourselves as
the heroes in history,
i remind myself that
they say there's two sides to a coin.
but, unfortunately i soon realised
this coin was made by you.

17. ugly

the mirror isn't my friend.
i walk past her,
stop to smile and play pretend.
without actually speaking,
she makes me feel ashamed.
and without actually moving,
she zooms in.
to show me all my flaws
and i must admit,
it pisses me off.
because i have other friends
who speak and don't make me feel ashamed.
who make me feel pretty
and will do so, again and again.
yet,
i can't help myself.
even when it's dark and there is nobody there,
i go back to the mirror
and stare.
even though the mirror isn't my friend,

i believe her
over the rest.

33

18. finding love

they told me you found love.
and i looked everywhere,
to find the one whose name you call,
last thing in the night
and first thing at first light.

but i couldn't find anything at all.
i looked up into the sky,
even looked between the stars.
And even looked to the dust
yet, i had no luck.

who is the one
that you have given all your love?
and when i asked you this
you answered, 'i carry His name on my tongue'
so i asked you where i could find him
and, instead of giving directions,
you gave me instructions
told me to cross my hands over my chest

and, steady myself.
put my mind to rest by
putting my forehead to the floor,
told me to call Him
and that was all.
the one you love,
i found within the fabrics of my being
and very soul.

19. my favourite colour

i like the colour brown.
it's my favourite colour.
i like the way
brown clothes suit my skin.
i like the way
brown is my skin,
how it outshines our gold.
i like my tea the same colour,
the same colour
as my tea bag-stained skin.
i like brown,
because it reminds me
of the richness of soil,
the richness within
my mother's eyes,
a cup of tea,
and autumn leaves.
if this colour was a person,
they would have the warmest hugs,

and bring you comfort.
brown is my favourite colour.

37

20. islamophobia

oh i am so sorry.
i do apologise, that you feel uncomfortable.
nothing to do with my behaviour
but, in your eyes
all muslims are the same.
and the muslim you saw on the news,
i must be the same, right?

yet, i do not see your white skin
and ask you,
why you colonised
because my eyes
see you before seeing your skin;
don't look at the exterior
because what matters is what's within.
and within you,
only exists ignorance.

because every time i smile,
at a white person,

i convince myself it's out of niceness
yet, i cant help
feel like i'm proving myself.
showing you i'm not a threat.
but, i can't help
when i notice you look me up and down
like, iv'e given you a reason to be scared of me.

all i did was smile
but yes, i am so sorry,
for your own ignorance
that makes you so scared of me.

21. grandma's garden

my grandma's garden.
my grandma's plants are fed, watered and loved.
she cares for them,
the same love she gave us.
the same hands
that pick and plant,
that picked and raised us,
hold so much love.

my grandma's garden is a reflection of her love,
how it shines, blooms and colours.
and us grandchildren
come from her garden of love.